WEATHER INVENTIONS

AKRON SERIES IN POETRY

AKRON SERIES IN POETRY
Mary Biddinger, Editor

Emily Rosko, *Weather Inventions*
Emilia Phillips, *Empty Clip*
Anne Barngrover, *Brazen Creature*
Matthew Guenette, *Vasectomania*
Sandra Simonds, *Further Problems with Pleasure*
Leslie Harrison, *The Book of Endings*
Emilia Phillips, *Groundspeed*
Philip Metres, *Pictures at an Exhibition: A Petersburg Album*
Jennifer Moore, *The Veronica Maneuver*
Brittany Cavallaro, *Girl-King*
Oliver de la Paz, *Post Subject: A Fable*
John Repp, *Fat Jersey Blues*
Emilia Phillips, *Signaletics*
Seth Abramson, *Thievery*
Steve Kistulentz, *Little Black Daydream*
Jason Bredle, *Carnival*
Emily Rosko, *Prop Rockery*
Alison Pelegrin, *Hurricane Party*
Matthew Guenette, *American Busboy*
Joshua Harmon, *Le Spleen de Poughkeepsie*

Titles published since 2010.
For a complete listing of titles published in the series, go to www.uakron.edu/uapress/poetry.

WEATHER
INVENTIONS

Emily Rosko

The University of Akron Press
Akron, Ohio

Copyright © 2018 by The University of Akron Press
All rights reserved • First Edition 2018 • Manufactured in the United States of America.
All inquiries and permission requests should be addressed to the publisher,
The University of Akron Press, Akron, Ohio 44325-1703.

ISBN: 978-1-629220-96-3 (paper)
ISBN: 978-1-629220-97-0 (ePDF)
ISBN: 978-1-629220-98-7 (ePub)

Library of Congress Cataloging-in-Publication Data
  Names: Rosko, Emily, 1979– author.
Title: Weather inventions / Emily Rosko.
Description: First edition. | Akron, Ohio : The University of Akron Press, 2018. |
  Series: Akron series in poetry |
Identifiers: LCCN 2017051218 (print) | LCCN 2017054841 (ebook) |
  ISBN 9781629220970 (ePDF) | ISBN 9781629220987 (ePub) | ISBN 9781629220963
  (paper : alk. paper)
Classification: LCC PS3618.O84425 (ebook) | LCC PS3618.O84425 A6 2018 (print) |
  DDC 811/.6—dc23
LC record available at https://lccn.loc.gov/2017051218

∞The paper used in this publication meets the minimum requirements of ANSI/NISO
z39.48–1992 (Permanence of Paper).

Cover image: *Atmosphere No. 46*, detail. Courtesy of Ian Fisher and Robischon Gallery,
Denver, CO. Cover design by Amy Freels.

Weather Inventions was designed and typeset in Baskerville by Amy Freels and printed on
sixty-pound natural and bound by Bookmasters of Ashland, Ohio.

Contents

How thought the beauty of being   1

I.
Gossamer   5
Reverdie   6
Weathervane   7
At the Rise, a Turn   8
A Rarity   9
Condition Notes   10
Electromagnetic   11
Sea Change   12
Rainbow   13

II.
Sail   17
Not Need but the Sky Outright   18
Drone   22
Condition Notes   23
Hail   24
The Candescence   26
Encasement   27
Fern   29
Drought   30
Vortex   31
The Greenery Goldens, Night Takes from Us All Forms   32

III.
Rain Devices   35
Condition Notes   37
Windmill   38
Tendered   39

Jet Stream 41
Transit 42
Hunted 43
Arrow 44
HAARP 45
Harvester 46

IV.
Cloud Study 49

V.
Condition Notes 57
Color Theory 58
Arctic 59
If Matters Come to the Worst, As in the Present Instance 60
Out of the Blue 62
Snowflake 64
Internal Compass 65
Uplands, Winter 67
Wind Aflush in the Head, A Wakefulness 68
Flood Plain 69
I Felt Like the Sound of a Harp 70

The Prevailing 73

Notes 75
Acknowledgments 79

How thought the beauty of being

and the difficult spaces in between.
Being here beautifies the thought:

the form of such things!
A tulip: singular instrument

of color, symmetry, organ, function;
a lure to the eye and the bee.

Thought from beneath all questions why:
bulb deep in earth, puzzling itself

into its made flower. An invisible
form of intention willed

by chance conditions: soil,
rainwater, air. How beauty is

thought into being: the wonder starting
out, between the winds lived in.

I

Gossamer

An unsolved riddle, a medieval poet said:
        this wake of moon disturbed

on the water, veil of angels fallen
        on Mary at the Assumption. Mornings,

the rose vines are threaded
        over; the meadow turned

to doily work, gauze and dew.
        It's the tiniest of aeronauts:

spinnerets sending up thread to air
        until it catches enough

to lift the spiderlings. Undulations
        of light, red to silver. Points of star-

burst gleaming with newness.
        This body of ascendant

hundreds will rise and fall the currents,
        wayward winded, dividing

the day to segments
        and whims. All chances

numbered, and such unreal
        possibility the leaves

uncount, sewn tree
        to tree. Each line

of pristine silk the marvel of
        we wake to see.

Reverdie

Call back spring and the migrations
of birds. Winter has sheared
down the birches to kindling
and ash, but from the gray
the new green budding. Call
back the spring, if spring
is still a season: zephyr winds
to calm the northerlies, the ground
defrosting and opening
to dew. Spiders spin
their filthy lacey
strings. Spring unrolls
a muddy field: the fecundity
of clay, golden pollen
sensualizing the air. Shower-burst
and thickened xylems. The up-
thrusted oozing nectar
sweetening the ongoing
infidelities of the bees. We'll
lie in the meadow, press flesh-
to-flesh against the damp warming
dirt, next to the earthworm
deconstructing all remains.
The grass unstitches to seed. Sky
a misted gauze that makes
no promise for what's planted or buried.

Weathervane

A reminder for denial: turning away
        from the sun, witness to the horizon's

crimson-streaked strife and blustery
        gales. Every steeple topped

by the cockerel: the one
        eye to the wind, whether fair

or foul. Feathered tail
        a warrior's flag, signaling the news

from on high: whether favor
        or fury. Divine sentence scripted

of conditionals. Noble fowl, gilded
        rooster, there is no morning song

to issue. You divide the sky to function
        and faith with compass points defaced.

You must tolerate the turbulence
        of what will pass by.

At the Rise, a Turn

A rusting plough for the field
                to overtake: a new ethic.

Chisel-work of rain: oxidation honeycombs
                the surface. The land is shaped

into strangeness; we are made to readjust
                our sight. Everything the plants know

                is weather-tempered, the bees'
experience wind-driven by spectra and unfolding

                sound. Overhead,
cloud intervals widen the afternoon:

                an abundance to reside in, layered
by the old traditions of wonder.

                Who ever said, "Extraordinary
                          facts teach us nothing"?

A Rarity

But the world, at the start, was bare: a mineral
        silence except for the wind translating
the particles. The atmosphere an artifact

        seeping from the crust's fissures:
the plumes surfacing as glass
        and sediment, the air a prism of heat.

Then, the eventual mixing: methane,
        ammonia, water vapor, carbon
dioxide (substance without form) converting

        sun to cells, oxidizing. Yet still,
the world was ashen, toneless
        except for the wind written in silver

on the water. In the shallows, a green
        algaic matter becoming a lung: drawing in,
releasing. A flourishing then—the marsh's

        pluff mud, sulfur by-product and decay
tempering the ozone from flare-ups. The air's
        elemental turmoil regulating

to patterns of clouds and currents. A first
        possible world ripening under this
enfolding membrane: the only blue to earth us.

Condition Notes

At first breath, a temperament embedded,
a guide in the ear:

    "that within us stands from our mouth downward."

The prehistoric bird in me gauges pressure
by the drum. A head

cotton-stuffed, cumulonimbi violet
at storm edge. Streamlined,

the tulip poplar's leaves pulled into
cylinders (a defense). First

marvel, then record. No other method,
I take note. In such winds, such blue.

Electromagnetic

Disruptions in the florid sky:

slight shifts, solar flares,
an early new heat to the day.

The clouds move in
shapes difficult to describe:

arrowy shadows, color
like a thought that grows.

We translate the patterns into
prophecy, train the eye to read

the signs the animals supply:
how the birds divide

the sky. Yet, even before the trees
(their greenery capsized

by the upswell of wind),
announce the storm,

an inner weather grows
out of the atmosphere's

ionic charge and every
molecule in us aware.

Sea Change

Turbulent presence,
                (who has seen?)

the wind's mosaics: triangular
crests, cat's-paws, the marbled

look of approach. Beneath
the sand, black rock

pocked, brittle as any
roughly handled thing. Weather-

worsted sea-bank, purple jellies
strewn petal-like. Capillary to white-

cap: spillover from a gale's
fetch. The water throws

diamonds neither you nor I
can count. A passing note,

when exhale becomes exalt
(it whirleth about continually).

The shallows drawn aside:
a fluke, a dividing of

the Gulf of Suez. Disobedient
form, "to imagine is to see."

Rainbow

Little lyric, little bunny-hopper
of song and throat. Little
whisper-wind. I call to you,
you me, and we are
communally distanced. You
have me by the string; I, you
by a raindrop's eye. Little vane,
little index. Paper-mache
of the inverse and
reverse. Double delight.
Nonsense. Roses at the gate.

II

Sail

Trade routes:

>   Night, the troposphere traversed
>   by insects and spiders on a silk
>
>   line. Wind-prone
>   specks: relinquished, wingless.

Our passage is

>   not the quickest, not end to
>   end, but wayward. Fish-scale
>
>   textures, the cloudfront, engendering
>   breeze, shift, the slip past.

Not Need but the Sky Outright

Paris, December, 1783. The first manned gas balloon flight by Jacques Charles and Nicholas Louis Robert.

1

The ground was well-traversed, each mountain
summit marked, coastlines drawn. Some depths
too had been achieved. But now, the atmosphere,
now to lift the body to heights with the fall
of all sound. We could rise by hemp and silk,
wicker and wire, by gas heat pulsing aflame
a chambered organ. The balloon's globe
centered the sky. It dizzied us from both sides
looking up, looking down. Rivers' scripted
curves, folds of treetops, vegetation in farmers'
fields. The lines of stone walls that enclosed
property, towns. We could go anywhere
the wind favored: no country
boundaries, all the unclaimed above.

2

To survey, first the eye must
grow accustomed to the turning

perspective, then one must stand
leaning over the edge penciling

the topography: the first look
above the unorganized cities, plotted

hectares, palace towers, church spires.
Ascent swells the eye

to all-seeing: the aeronaut
mythic with dominion

over the microscopic people left
on the ground. What vantage

of the ongoing world! the unfathomed
textures! Time thins, the air ices

the lungs. The realms one beholds
from nowhere in the zeroed blue.

3

Seeing from below, the limits.

Once, above the cloudscape, the world looked patterned:
serpentine veins of river, tributaries,

farm-fielded hilltops. We had never before been
this way, positioned with an inverse gaze;

our selves tinier than before and partially
lost in the atmospheric haze. No one could know

us here or here. We had to stand so still.
We realmed out time, and time was

not contingent and space was wide.

A cold clarity felt nowhere. When we landed back
aright, grounded, our bodies weighed

more. We had much to tell. And tried.
Our feet sank in mud. The closeness

of wool to our skin. Part of us rose
up great, scientific. Part never returned.

4

The balloon's flight chanced open
the sky with possibilities. Designs
were hatching. Many thought our lives

reinvented, that cities would exist
floating in the utopic blue, that the marvel
would bring us closer

to God's eye. But we were still
ourselves, with no new ideas
save the old ones: how to move armies

across the channel, how to keep watch
of enemies. We could see and record all
so that nothing would ever surprise us again.

Drone

The images are precise and anonymous.

Bodies and objects are enlarged by their shadows.

One shadow shows running.

You cannot tell age or expression so well,

but there is no doubt when there is a crowd.

Such as the numbers bent head to ground in prayer.

The symmetry of the suburbs is striking.

So, too, the cars parked

within their white lines, a pattern of herringbone.

Sun-blanked windshields. The ongoing asphalt.

The agriculture is immense, especially the exposed cattle pens

stocked with most facing the same direction.

The lands with nothing. The nothing land.

The clearest days mean the most harm.

Condition Notes

A reversal in the works,
      the sun a failure of dissolve,

ice shelves minimizing mass. A slip-sure
      movement, a terrain that's due

to float differently—erratic, self-motivated.
      "Water astonishing and difficult

altogether makes a meadow and a stroke."
      Not some joke, no safe canoe.

Hail

Form is determined
by air temperature and cloud
      layers. The sky obscured so that all sky

is nimbus: layers, bands, a hazy
turbidness, sheeted and we are
      lost in it, imperfect to see.

Snow-full, heavy with icelets
that gravity pulls down.
      The architecture never holds—

cumulonimbus tip to downpour.
The vapors merge,
      break, merge, evaporate,

collide with an upsweep
to freeze, refreeze as hailstone.
      A precise frenzy: a chemistry,

drafting a physical formation
no hand can mix or draw.
      Instability makes the rain

fall. Morning mists, drizzles.
The mutability of clouds
      as difficult to figure as God—

nothing preserved or absolute. No
strategy to gain access, no force
      or plea. We go

too easily from awe
to fear. Oceanic traffic
      of the heavens and us unarmed.

The Candescence

Europe, the summer of 1783, when extreme atmospheric disturbances followed a series of strong volcanic eruptions in Iceland and Japan.

Great numbers were carried off,
and those who stayed wept to see

the meat spoil in cellars and unnerved
horses stamp eddies in the dirt. Flies

hatched quick, thick in unmoving
air. There was a dim and wary eye

cast heavenward, louring red and veiled
not by dust alone, but horizons riven

by fog, contagion. Electrical storms
forked fires. Reported tremors. Rust-

colored, damp light shaded
the ground. By whose will are we meant

to suffer so? Those who stayed sought
the spoil to weep the earth's upheavals,

our sickly selves fallen far. The whole
of sky white above, sun a hazed ball

thought away. Rain cancelled the crops.
June, from trees the leaves shed. Here,

a time unexampled. Here, lettered
the same dispirited experience: the world

was not ours. It grew dark. The dark of ash
and sulfur, a blot settled sure within.

Encasement

A husk—here so long

      as noontides pull. A humming-

            bird's weight: unscaled

                  fright. Ruby-throated, backward-

going: an escapist's illusionary

trick. So the soul sits high

            angle right, balanced in a peculiar

      geometry. "Some kind of letters

                  are good squares others hand-

      some ovals." Circuitous,

a season spent in frigid

            wrappings: gauze turned

      guise. The bulb's compactness, leaves

                                        fleshing the trees.

        A trade, a small gust,

                                once it goes, it goes out—

Fern

Even as inside
as you are, you are
not yet inly enough.

I know you with your
folding in: the start of
the fern frond, snail-tight

curl, the whisk and horse-
tail which unrolls a quick-
scaled green-forming,

uncoils its scrollwork
of fiddlehead, shepherd's
crook which seeks

the ground, no seed or
flower to concentrate
on, even as in shade

and poor soil it thrives:
only you go the other
way: tighter knot, false

part of unfurling. Sink
to dirt a deeper bed
those roots, my love.

Drought

Though the wind takes its cut through
the ambered, tired leaves trees
can barely hold onto, there is little
to let go of. Once, I was full of sap
and starched greenness to tend
the garden, until you took to sharpening

your teeth as the rain-manic
squirrels do in high August when water's
sponged in the clouds. Then
your rot took hold underneath; had all
exposed and gripped as hide
and bone could not guard

against ruin. Such sun-blasted
nonsense you were! Dust
and solar flare storms. Ozone thawed
the arctic. Lakes unfed, and beds the residue
of salt my hands matched. Pines long-needled
for tinder. Your marks unreason

the sky, blind with glare. Off you go,
the winds say, hurrying you to raze
the fields of some future's undoing.

Vortex

I'm sorry to report
                passing

ropelike, conditions
amazingly throughout

fit for/of
microburst,

scud cloud
incorrectly filler

flanking line of
swell

        completion
        (standard moves, reflections)

squall turned gust turned mesocyclonic

thunder-crack, sea
surge, waterspout—
                reversal

of lake, conduction from inside out:

retreat, the skinned soft ground

The Greenery Goldens,
Night Takes from Us All Forms

We are minded to ourselves. A closing
in: banded in broad skeletal, self-

ruining organizations. Tossed about.
Solitary form surrounded by blue.

A small voice of regret. This gazing up
and up; this watch for change, for

the next spectacle. The above mirrors
itself on bodies of water. Impressionistic:

a camel, a weasel, a whale. An orchestration
of parts: our singular cold, distempered hearts.

Some watching tells doom, some the promise
of rain; yet, some take the skies wholly

summed. An unlasting state: our final
looking ever upward, our tendency to not.

III

Rain Devices

Shake open the sky for rain, bells,
and cannons. Trumpets to startle

drops on the deforested, parched
plains. Release the kites with electrical

charges, the balloons packed
with dynamite to effect a concussion

of air. Results: impervious. Atmosphere
undrained. Build next a high tower

and summon rain from chemical
gases as teakettle vapors swirl.

Change the conditions to attract
moisture—desert heat to tropical

deluges. A delusion. A shift to new
technology: crop dusters loaded

with insecticides, engineered
aircraft targeting clouds. Attempt

to disperse the mass of water
vapors, drop sand to seed, drop

dry ice pellets to form a cloud chamber
of crystals. Results: snow. Prompt

the scientists and strategists to test
possibilities further. Weaponize

low visibility, the downpour: silver
iodide to oil the clouds. Monsoons

to landslide a war. Profit from fresh
powder in the mountains, relieve

drought for the desperate, divert
the hurricane's course. Results:

precipitation *here* means none *there*,
all fluid dynamics thrown off.

Under no imperatives will it rain.

Condition Notes

A manipulation of appearances—skies

take to burning salmon-copper

at the horizon line: a warning

the day ends with ourselves over-

measured and sick from the bloom.

Azaleas in loud pink-

throatedness, small tongues

full of show. We dwell within

gauge and pressure. We do not give

out names lightly: *bright forecast, royal*

command, conversation piece, twenty grand.

Our inventions are wont to be pretty toys;

we are distracted from serious things.

Windmill

To amplify the good forces,
flags and prayer wheels wind-activated.
A ceremony of rotation
to send out sacred mantras

via the great floodgates
of the wonder-world. To catch
the vertical winds' drag to pump
water, Persia's first

panemone. To blade the propeller,
feather with reeds;
then, canvas sails reefed
into dagger points

to mill the corn. To open
and close in sync
with gust speeds, wooden
shutters. To pivot,

a post. To signal
from hilltop the news, station
the arms: cross
or X for tax collectors or

death. To the industry
of the drained wetlands!—
paper and threshing,
wool and seed oils, paints

and stone. To reap
the wind's labor, each turn
a gain in momentum; the
shifty sky polished white.

Tendered

Everything invented we pay
or die for: the sky's white erase

mark the jet plane makes

of the blue-worn slate. A drama
to state the bridges know

how to fall. The corn's slack,

green, straw-fiber leaf planted,
army in mind. Tin traded

for time, bunkered in by noon's

stock and draw. There is no one
eye to follow: the sightline

limits the horizon. Disaster's

soil-amended, engineered to
bond chemical component

to irised insect wing. In the park,

where we walk our lives in rounds
to size the cartoonish flowers'

growth, the ginkgo's rate of falling

yellow leaves from start to end,
the Citadel cadets set trained

riflescopes on us to where we are

edged by pretend fire. The dog,
too, point-wary. Their positioned

bodies, faces of no exchange.

Jet Stream

Urgency was behind the wind's study.

A calculation, rate of diffusion.

From on low, incendiary, Tokyo, swept.

Intermingling systems, a polar-front current.

Hydrogen balloons crossing the Pacific eastward.

One to Michigan intact, one to Oregon not.

We sent back two suns.

Transit

The night Venus shouldered by
the sun, we all witnessed the way
desire cuts between us. No more

fickle than a monarch flitting zinnia
head to head, the marked-out path
is one long-known. Never before

has prophecy seemed so underestimated.
Everything measured, orbital, bracing itself
around the one fool truth the sun unmakes

in its solar flare-ups. We are semi-short
of grandeur. We divide time
to capital-marked quantities, which end

in some bodily pain, in a form
this language cannot even contain. Gods,
there are no short-cuts. The flowering

plants wiped clean of earth-known
remedies. Bodies heated with friction,
the magnetic pull of opposites: love to hate.

The crowds wait for brutality and collision.
What the sword-bent powers take
are not answers to mind but signs to sear

the cursive of catastrophe in clay. Here,
much is soft—that's why we are so threat-full,
so sure terror is ours to brandish and bear.

Hunted

The difficulties started small.
Most sounds from the hollows of pine
forest muffled. The ground twitched
a bit, at the outset: a bending back
of branches the deer would never
break. Air tensed. So, the birds. Catcall

of squirrels. Oh, the difficulties were small,
it seemed, but not a blot or a remarkable note
upon the day. The ferns, though, journaled it
all—their leaves flattened by footfalls.
We have no fears but the animal ones.
The clouds bone-fished to scrape out sun

from the blue; ozone overripe with rot
and fruit. The edge of everything grew
edgier. Did I say the difficulties were
small, at first? I could have bedded
myself a grave to dirt; I was outside
the periphery, not under shot but within

aim. Honeysuckle overtook, the scrub-berries
reddened. The forest turned itself to secret
green, each leaf folded meanness down
to the root. Many soft bodies moved through
at night. Bats in swoop to carve the air
of insects. The screech owl mole-hunted:

the pierce of its catch that made
our ears the worst instrument. One
we cannot move away from for any good.

Arrow

A war, or
a slain row
of sirs, gents,

grandsons, now garlands.
Again, the liar's snow:
a snarl of wording.

Low in the grassland,
suffering. A frost
the awns sharpen.

Furlongs drawn to rift
the fir-sawn gruffness,
a ruth-torn stringer. Oh,

this word sings
the narrows raw, or
inward snags organs

whole. Worse, laws
the songster: owl
to swan. I ungreen this

tree with thorn. Rough-
run the hunt, draw
in tear and air.

HAARP

        (High-frequency Active Auroral Research)

In Alaska, some say, "skies are being programmed"

by a vast field of phased-array antenna beaming
        radio waves upward to excite particles

        in the ionosphere. It creates an auroral electroject: small
percent of solar irradiance, positioned as natural

currents flow from north to south poles, circling. A path
        from a noon to midnight sun. Patterns

        of modulated heat. The hoped-for effects:
improved communication with air and underwater

navigation and the ability to map terrestrial subsurfaces
        for minerals and underground complexes.

        Yet, the science is beyond us, triggering a cascade
of findings and warnings that "the planet will capsize"

as magnetic poles flip. Others say it brews super-storms,
        supplies access to read our brains. Weather-

        force tactics again. We can cite
the polar mesospheric summer echoes that exist above

the noctilucent clouds, can make the luminous glow
        of artificial ionosphere—first human-made aurora

        visible to plain eye. Such power is not effective
to counter the magnitude of damages from burning out our only sky.

All particles undone to cosmic whispers and hum.

Harvester

When the sunset's a mess of pastels
retreating, you'll lose

yourself to a forgotten autumn

where the heads of the flowers
curl up inside their own

crown to become a faint

thought inside the dropped
seed. Papery leaves, sluggish bees.

So this is splendor, this is slippage:

an abundance the trees can't
perfect, quick to thin as they do.

Blighted stems, the splotched zinnias:

remainders half-open. And the pale
moths that encircle them, each

bringing the message to be the last.

IV

Cloud Study

—After John Constable

    1

What might be called accuracy,
later, truth—
in the space between realms,
more had risen.
The atmosphere preoccupied
with thinking: a repeated
conclusion: open sky, region
of the cirrus, rain-cloud.
None better invented.

2

A motif: lastingness in the unending
sequence. The sky became true
over two brief summers. Effects of light
writ small. From the village
to the meadow all our gestures
measured nostalgia. Buttercups, clover:
unified fieldwork. The trials
of the eye to catch the dissolving clouds.

And then—   (nothing truly seen)

3

The brilliant crucible of paint: OXIDE
OF MANGANESE, PROTIODIDE OF MERCURY,

SESQUIOXIDE OF CHROMIUAM. Nevertheless
limited, even thinned down. The sky

refused to obey with its migrations
of tint, form, shadow. Aerial expanses

without history. Nowhere
exists in the storehouse of clouds.

4

To furnish the canvas with correspondences:
the sunset over the Thames thrown vivid
by volcanic eruptions. Streaky clouds at
the horizon. Half-cloud, half-plain.

A competent idea of a volcano, waterspout, wind.
Outward manifestations are attempts.

5

Relying on nature for its measure:
the science of painting the sky
lectures the imagination's sketch ability—
blue and white as scraps of paper.

Having suffered, having observed reality…

Noted: "Showery Wind N. Easterly."
The standard of scale, the sky as a page
overtaken with oddities of light,
from excess to wisp—

the weather of the clouds an endlessly
recursive system of signs.

V

Condition Notes

A weakness in the sky.

Nothing overstretched or bent,

but crumpled perhaps, as the brain.

No high calls from treetops this morning.

A darted body or two, an instrument of conditionals.

Look to survey, look to reduce.

Look to be something other.

Arctic weatherwall that approaches.

Cirrus handspun in the sky's top layer.

Calm decline, this wait.

Something everything else is good at.

The rose canes' purple flush.

The evergreens with their name.

Color Theory

Green as the absence: the leaves a pigment
other than sun. Reflection is selective,
assumptions the eye holds. Color waved through
lengths, earth-bound chemistry. Spectral

minerals: the orange to flame iron-red
berry in the wings of insects, the cardinal
alit on the fir branch heavied by snow.
It catches us by mistake, the inner

outer showing. Iris-wide. We take blue
for the mover: the sapphire-plated,
soulish-something the sky. Dark fading
to the faintest possible pale

of atmosphere, right at the edge of space's
midnight, we lose ourselves past seeing.

Arctic

The front topples and the draft pours in
on the inhabitants. The shift a quick
plummet. The physics of it: division
and discontinuity. A correction: a fluid
feeding, winds shearing molecule against
molecule. We have so much to endure. Precise
iced night. Stars hard-dotted. Every shadow
permanent on the pavement. The burrowing
creatures sink in deeper. The birds stilled
in their slight legs and song. We are cold
to begin with. Mineral cold, earthed by
a body primed for defense.

If Matters Come to the Worst, As in the Present Instance

A scalloped-out blue shell. The sky's sliced
by the hawk on the scour, the little

sun, shadows the creatures
hide in, under leaf, against the rock's

dull cold. What's the difference
between the tree stoic against the cloudfront

and the arcing trace the early moon makes?
I do not know what the leaves will take,

their wrist-skin upturned to wind. I do
not know what anger will come. Nothing beyond

what small self I have, resolute as stones
bedded under the river current. I am no

longer feeling but all feeling, the softness
in me the softness in others and inside

the center faulted. Cracked ribcage to
collar. The afterstorm atmosphere

emptied of anything held by the bone-
bare tree, sycamore mottled, each twig

unleafed by their dream of spring. Each
of us in a perfect unloveliness we all

know but do not mention. No one
should be afraid, the stars say wheeling

out their hard separation, unwilled
in their staying, in their one small pin-

pierce that holds all the dark nothing away.

Out of the Blue

When it all turns to dust
> *And turn to dust it shall*

The ground a sigh long-exhaling
> *All exhales grounded*

Out from the mineral-white marl
> *The marl of shells, white*

We have learned little of things
> *The things we littled*

And over time the world's forgotten
> *And have forgotten*

We underskied the heavens
> *The sky evens*

Grew weary and heavy, animal-stoic
> *A burden grown elephantine*

Against what calling is heard,
> *Returned a voice calling*

What stillness in the turning
> *That turned us*

From summer noon to none
> *Nothing of nooned summer*

Although we are lost to begin with
> *Will stay us*

Crowned, haloed by faults
> *A halo of faults as a crown*

Footed so
> *And footed so*

We go as dust to the ground
> *To ground, to dust we go*

Snowflake

and then something
        raised up   a wind inside

wherever space is
        —bell, hand, tulip, crown—

magnetized between two
        chambers   a conveyance

an internal climate of the body
        when a *tree trunk becomes a feeling*

turbulent, the charged ground
        of grass accordion-bent

("accidents, events")
        so this makes spindle

and arrow, net-veined as
        the dragonfly   ("a resemblance to

an animal in a starlet of snow")

Internal Compass

—in good spirits when (it did not rain there)

I was there. A formality to get through, clocked
as a knotted rope,

                                        disturbance of air
                                            caused by

heat (indexed and recorded), the range
of electrical potential

                                        a semantic shift

bated by leafshake. There, a margin the trees
did not cover,

                                        a windflaw, a stroke—

opening what I thought
room for nasturtium (radial, spurred open)

                                        for so long facing south,
                                            for so long north.

Put to ground, fears
are sometimes uneven, because

                                        in a sense the weather
                                          does change

dusk sharpens the afternoon with passing
cloud lines. Gray-

                                        then slips, falls, then

pink intensities (all the time
there is this)

                                        keeps the calm.

Uplands, Winter

Catch: the morning's sky went
falling, crystalline clumps
snowheaped.

Firs coated white. In between,
gray. In between the stillness
that might be time

measured for sight. I was quiet most
hours. Heart's pulse. A certain
nothing to mind.

Rabbit tracks print
the yard. Buried woodpile.
Each shiver

and shrink of the old house has been
felt. Mice nesting in
the walls. Some shuffler

boots his way to some car. Some
dour face. Some of
a heaviness.

Could the day change, it won't.
Minus the blue, the gold the sky:
a solid permanence.

At noon, the bell out on the hill
drowned itself under
a train whistle.

No other sounds
to startle. No startling thought
but here and here and here.

Wind Aflush in the Head, A Wakefulness

The cold winds feelingly persuade
me what I am. Temporary
wakefulness that shakes
the mind as if a forest canopy, darkly
flushed and increasing. The late sky's
cirrus is spent. Wind-billowed, cauterized
cloud-ribs remain. Dogwood buds
button-closed against the in-breaking
sun. Bone-gray branches
but all the limbs alive. This air
in me is not me but I inhabit
it. Every breath, a threshold.

Flood Plain

I'd like to go on as if there's no end.
One vast

causeway to the ocean. All the
unsolved bits

as gold pressed into stone.
Solar-flash,

false capture. Sky like glass
on the water.

Here, then there, then back to a never-
again. When

the spidery clouds take up the radiance
in colors

severe with impermanence;
when the maple

along the avenue is bird-filled, a ruckus
of song and

flurry, there will be a softening,
some release:

surface winds will switch the leaves
to silver (a ripple

of creaturely breathing); snow-melt
will animate the stream; and

the grazing grounds will wash out over
broad stones.

I Felt Like the Sound of a Harp

and all else
wind-strung. Seed pinwheels
of the oak, airplane propellers

dividing the air
in spring. A sound the ear
cannot catch; nor the mind

bending back to afternoons
of anyplace else. I could have
sat in the sun-patch all day.

The tulips in agreement.
The unmarvelled cocoons
twined in the firs and sumac.

I have not thought of this
in some time. Circling
the house for signs:

robin shells, fist-sized
young rabbits, snails,
the short red nub of new

leaf on the roses. I do not
know the air, but I do. I'm ever
so unsure it was all

here. The day divided
by grass blades, some green
thing bounding up the soil.

Clouds sweeping by
in a hurry, the blue with
no place else to go.

The Prevailing

In arctic rivers, a vortex
patterning air currents pole to pole. And the wind was

the first stirring, the planet suffering cosmic gales.
Mountains riveted, and the wind erased the edges:

quartz to grit, the shifting pieces of the immutable
made fluid. And the wind polished curves

in sandstone: dunes resculpted crescent
to crescent. The wave-swell's tuft of white, oxygen

folded into sea foam. Then the gilled creatures, then
the lung ungilling. Balloon-chambered tissue, arteries

uptaking the parts of air to heart, brain, appendage,
and the sudden new way of weeping. And,

wildflowers stirred to wildness, the winged seeds
sent out by maple and ash and the plumed

seeds (the air near flowering) of willow, thistle,
daisy, and bulrush. And the uncountable insects

with an architecture of veined wings: prismatic,
fringed, stenciled, transparent. Airfoils that shape

the body, set it abuzz, the motion a figure eight.
Microscopic particles the wind is seeped in: a biome

of viruses and protozoans, the flurry we reside in.
And the wind placed our cities, and we built to keep it

out of our houses. And the wind was often against us,
and we named our winds our gods. Reeds

feathered and sharpened, the strung-sharp arrow
of the wind played to notes. And the throat, too, a wind

instrument, and the wind funneled through brass
valves and pipes. And we instructed the wind

to turn the blades. And we made the wind
carry us—by sail and thrust. And the wind's work

brittles us to remains: skin to bone swept dry
to some airy substance whence we first were.

Notes

"Gossamer": It was Geoffrey Chaucer who called gossamer "an unsolved riddle."

"Weathervane": A cock atop a church spire is said to represent Peter's denial of Christ. Inspired by Alexandra Harris's *Weatherland: Writers & Artists Under English Skies* (New York, NY: Thames & Hudson, 2015).

"At the Rise, a Turn": "This 'Tradition of Wonder' represented a backlash against the disenchantment of nature inaugurated by the new sciences, a tradition of just celebrating—not trying to explain—the strange, the surprising, the awesome, and the wonderful" (Vladimir Janković, *Reading the Skies: A Cultural History of English Weather, 1650–1820*. Chicago: University of Chicago Press, 2000), 41.

Condition Notes: "At first air, a temperament embedded": Line in quotations from a Diné creation song (James Kale McNeley, *Holy Wind in Navajo Philosophy*. Tucson, AZ: University of Arizona Press, 1981).

"Electromagnetic": A few lines and language from sections VIII and IX of Wallace Stevens's "The Man With the Blue Guitar" are enfolded in this poem.

"Sea Change": Christina Rossetti, "Who Has Seen the Wind?"; "The wind goeth toward the south, and turneth about unto the north; it whirleth about continually, and the wind returneth again according to his circuits" (Hebrew Bible, *Ecclesiastes* 1:6); Andre Breton, "to imagine is to see."

"Not Need but the Sky Outright": Facts on the history of ballooning come from Richard Holmes's *Falling Upwards: How We Took to the Air* (New York, NY: Pantheon Books, 2013).

"Drone": After photographs by Tomas van Houtryve.

Condition Notes: "A reversal in the works": The sentence in quotation marks belongs to Gertrude Stein.

"The Candescence": During the summer of 1783, England and much of the Continent experienced extreme atmospheric disturbances as the result of several severe, sequential volcanic explosions in Japan in December 1782 and in Iceland in June 1783.

"Encasement": "Some kind of letters are good squares others handsome ovals…" taken from Keats's letter to J. H. Reynolds [Teignmouth, May 3, 1818] from *English Romantic Writers*, ed. David Perkins, 2nd ed. (New York, NY: Harcourt Brace & Co.,1995), 1280.

"Rain Devices": Indebted to Cynthia Barnett's *Rain: A Natural and Cultural History* (New York, NY: Crown Publishers, 2015).

Condition Notes: "A manipulation of appearance": The final two lines are based on a quote by Henry David Thoreau.

"Windmill": "The great floodgates of the wonder-world" belongs to Herman Melville. Lyall Watson's *Heaven's Breath: A Natural History of the Wind* (New York, NY: William Morrow and Company, Inc., 1984) supplied facts on the windmill's development.

"Jet Stream": The jet stream was discovered during World War II by the Japanese, who used the wind currents to carry helium balloons packed with explosives west to the United States.

"Arrow": An anagram poem using Shakespeare's words from *Hamlet*: "to suffer / The slings and arrows."

"HAARP": To get lost in the science and the surrounding conspiracy theories, just google "HAARP."

"Cloud Study": John Constable (1776-1837) was one of the first to apply the discoveries of the developing sciences to painting. His work relied on Luke Howard's popular and ground-breaking meteorological essay, "On the Modifications of Clouds" (1804). Constable's 1836 lecture on the history of landscape painting at the Royal Institution in London began with a statement that the profession of painting is "scientific as well as poetic; that imagination alone never did, and never can, produce works that are to stand by a comparison with reality" (Richard Hamblyn, *The Invention of the Clouds: How an Amateur Meteorologist Forged the Language of the Skies*. New York, NY: Farrar, Straus and Giroux, 2001). Attributed to the Buddha: "Nowhere exists in a storehouse of clouds."

"If Matters Come to the Worst, As in the Present Instance": Title from John Thelwall, *The Peripatetic; or Sketches of the Heart, of Nature and Society* (1793).

"Snowflake": Michel Serres, *La naissance de la physique dans le texte de Lucrèce* (Paris: Editions de Minuit, 1977), 85; Johannes Kepler, *The Six-Cornered Snowflake: A New Year's Gift* (1611), trans. Colin Hardie (Oxford: Clarendon Press, 1966). The italicized phrase "tree trunk becomes a feeling" comes from Myung Mi Kim's poem "405" in *Commons* (Oakland, CA: University of California Press, 2002).

"Wind Aflush in the Head, A Wakefulness": "The cold winds feelingly persuade me what I am" from Shakespeare's *As You Like It*.

"I Felt Like the Sound of a Harp": "I felt like the sound of a harp" is how one patient described the bodily sensations of elation that resulted from breathing in nitrous oxide during Humphry Davy's first experiments with the gas (Richard Holmes, *The Age of Wonder: How the Romantic Generation Discovered the Beauty and Terror of Science*. New York, NY: Vintage Books, 2008).

Acknowledgments

Thank you to the editors of the following literary journals where these poems, in their earlier forms, first appeared:

Aesthetix, Another Chicago Magazine, Antioch Review, Beloit Poetry Journal, Caffeine Destiny, Cimarron Review, Connotation Press: An Online Artifact, Denver Quarterly, Diode, Front Porch, The Missouri Review (online), *New American Writing, New Orleans Review, Pank, Pleiades,* and *Visible Binary.*

"Transit" was awarded first place in the 2016 Porter Fleming Literary Competition.

The various forces of many have buoyed the spirit of this book along the way. Thanks to the College of Charleston for providing a Research and Development grant toward the writing of this book, and thank you to the School of Humanities and Social Sciences for support as well.

This book would not be possible without Mary Biddinger and Amy Freels's fierce dedication and advocacy for poetry. My deepest thanks, too, to Jon Miller and the University of Akron Press Editorial Board.

Finally, with love to Anton and Elsa—first true wonder—who got a little bit of blue sky caught in her eye when she was born.

Photo: Anton Vander Zee

Emily Rosko is the author of two previous poetry collections: *Prop Rockery*, winner of the 2011 Akron Poetry Prize, and *Raw Goods Inventory*, winner of the 2005 Iowa Poetry Prize. She has been the recipient of the Stegner and Ruth Lilly fellowships. Editor of *A Broken Thing: Poets on the Line* (University of Iowa Press, 2011), she also is the poetry editor for *Crazyhorse*. She is associate professor of English at the College of Charleston.